FROM THE EDITORS OF *THE OFFICIAL JOHN WAYNE MAGAZINE*

EVERYTHING I NEED TO KNOW I LEARNED FROM

JOHN WAYNE

Duke's Solutions to Life's Challenges

"I'VE MADE OVER 250 PICTURES AND HAVE NEVER SHOT A MAN IN THE BACK. CHANGE IT."

—John Wayne, while objecting to a scene
in his last film, *The Shootist* (1976)

★ ★ ★

MY FATHER PLAYED many roles throughout his career, and while some characters certainly had their flaws, every single one was a person audiences could admire. Whether he was the Ringo Kid looking to avenge his father's death, Col. Mike Kirby leading his men into battle in Vietnam, or J.B. Books settling the last of his scores before saying goodbye for good—and refusing to shoot a man in the back in order to do so—Duke's signature honesty, loyalty and grit always shone through.

Duke lived his life by a code (a man's got to have one, after all), and the men he portrayed on-screen did as well. In this collection, you'll find more than 50 lessons pulled straight from John Wayne's films, as well as several quotes that stand as damn-good advice on their own. While it's true Duke cast a long shadow both figuratively and literally, there's no reason we can't all aspire to measure up to the example he left behind.

—ETHAN WAYNE

3

Duke shares a scene in 1969's *True Grit* with Kim Darby and Glen Campbell. The film is the only one for which John Wayne ever won an Academy Award.

Never Quit

We've all been told at one time or another that when the going gets tough, the tough get going. And while you may not consider yourself quite as tough as any of the rugged, seemingly fearless characters John Wayne portrayed on the big screen, the truth is everyone is capable of rising to the occasion. All it takes is the right mentality.

★ ★ ★

HE QUESTION "You wanna quit, Ethan?" posed by Capt. Rev. Samuel Clayton (Ward Bond) in *The Searchers* elicits the type of response you might expect from a John Wayne character. In the 1956 film, Duke's Ethan Edwards, a veteran of the American Civil War, devotes years of his life to the

mission of rescuing his niece Debbie (Natalie Wood) from her Comanche captors, even though the endeavor seems more fruitless with each passing year. "That'll be the day," Edwards replies, scoffing at the idea of ever calling it quits. Eventually, Edwards' attitude leads him and his crew to Debbie, validating the veteran's steadfast will to continue the quest.

It's a welcome reminder that even when the deck is stacked against you, success is still possible. Don't throw in the towel—grit your teeth and get it done.

Demand the Respect You Deserve

> "I WON'T BE WRONGED, I WON'T BE INSULTED
> AND I WON'T BE LAID A HAND ON.
> I DON'T DO THESE THINGS TO OTHER PEOPLE,
> AND I REQUIRE THE SAME FROM THEM."
>
> —J.B. BOOKS, *THE SHOOTIST* (1976)

★ ★ ★

IN JOHN WAYNE'S final film, *The Shootist*, he imparted a valuable lesson to audiences: Treat others how you wish to be treated, and don't put up with those who don't do the same. It's an aphorism we've all heard since we were children, yet too many people let such common courtesies fall by the wayside. But J.B. Books holds true to his convictions, even while knocking on death's door. It's an example the rest of us should follow, too.

You Can't Work Without Trust

Working with someone you don't know well can be difficult, especially when you're used to doing things your way. You might think your way is best, but sometimes, it's in the best interest of everyone to have a little trust and be a team player.

★ ★ ★

JOHN WAYNE'S character Wedge Donovan learns this lesson in unfortunate fashion in 1944's *The Fighting Seabees*. Leading a construction project in the Pacific during World War II, Donovan believes his men should be armed against incoming Japanese forces. This clashes with the orders of Lt. Commander Robert Yarrow (Dennis O'Keefe), Donovan's liaison officer who insists the Navy will protect the men. When Japanese forces arrive,

Donovan goes rogue and leads his construction crew into battle, unknowingly sabotaging Yarrow's well-laid strategy and leading to the deaths of many of Donovan's men.

You might not find yourself in such dire circumstances, but the lesson here remains the same: You need to be able to trust the people you're working with, even if you don't necessarily understand their reasons. Finding that trust together is part of what makes a job worth doing.

"WE BROUGHT NOTHING INTO THIS WORLD AND IT'S CERTAIN WE CAN CARRY NOTHING OUT."

★ ★ ★

—Thomas Dunson, *Red River* (1948)

Don't Tolerate Cheaters

John Wayne never took a shortcut in his life. His modest upbringing and determined ascent up the Hollywood ladder etched an appreciation of hard work and honest effort that never waned throughout his life. Those same virtues were often at the core of characters he portrayed on-screen.

★ ★ ★

N THE 1944 FILM *Tall in the Saddle*, Duke's ranch hand character, Rocklin, is new in town and soon discovers the denizens to be far from hospitable. When he plays a game of poker with a local, Rocklin catches the man playing an illegal card. The cheater pulls his gun when Rocklin reaches for the

winnings, but Rocklin keeps his cool and walks away. Moments later, he returns to the table, this time with his own gun holstered at his side. He looks the underhanded player in the eye and simply says, "I've come for my money." Clearly intimidated, the local apologizes and tries to explain himself, but Rocklin pays no regard and simply walks away with his winnings.

The scene teaches us that refusing to stoop to the lowdown ways of others has its rewards. In other words, stick to your guns—even if that means leaving them holstered.

Actions Have Consequences

> ## "BECAUSE NO MATTER WHERE PEOPLE GO, SOONER OR LATER THERE'S THE LAW."
>
> —JOHN CHISUM, *CHISUM* (1970)

★ ★ ★

UKE'S CHARACTER John Chisum in *Chisum* is not a man who would ever let geographical details get in the way of what needs to be done. The rugged cattle baron lets his sidekick James Pepper (Ben Johnson) know he's mistaken when Pepper recites an old saying: "There's no law west of Dodge and no God west of the Pecos." As far as Chisum sees it, justice knows no boundaries. And this lesson applies well beyond the realm of legalities and Western heroes and villains. You can't run from your problems—especially those you create for yourself.

Know When to Fight

It's always better to solve your problems with words and
to avoid unnecessary violence. But sometimes, when a fella just
can't be reasoned with (particularly if he throws the first punch),
a bit of violence may be just what the doctor ordered.

★ ★ ★

N 1952'S *THE QUIET MAN*, Duke plays Sean Thornton, a
retired boxer who has sworn to never raise his fists again. He
moves to Ireland to start over and reclaim his family farm, and
unexpectedly falls in love and marries Mary Kate, played by
Maureen O'Hara. But their marriage is marred by her brother Will's
disapproval and his refusal to pay her dowry. Thornton, who doesn't

understand how important the custom is to his wife, ignores the issue. But when his wife leaves him over the matter, enough is enough. Thornton goes to his brother-in-law and demands the dowry, winning his wife's respect. After Mary Kate leaves, Will takes a swing at Thornton, causing him to break his vow of peace and hit back. The ensuing fight becomes an epic brawl throughout the village—and Thornton wins that round, too.

Though Thornton had vowed he would never fight again, life doesn't always allow us to take the passive route. Some things are worth fighting for—figuratively and literally—and the respect of your partner and family definitely tops the list.

Whatever You're Doing, Do It Right

> **"YOU CAN'T GIVE THE ENEMY A BREAK. SEND HIM TO HELL."**
>
> —LT. COL. BENJAMIN VANDERVOORT, *THE LONGEST DAY* (1962)

★ ★ ★

WHETHER HE was acting, directing, parenting or just playing a game of chess, John Wayne always gave maximum effort. In *The Longest Day*, Duke's character Lt. Col. Benjamin Vandervoort expects the same from his fellow men in uniform before heading into battle. And since John Wayne was portraying an actual World War II hero in the film, his conviction is all the more palpable.

The many challenges life throws your way can feel like the enemy at times. Don't back down—give 'em all you've got.

"I GOT A BAD HABIT OF TELLIN' THE TRUTH, BUT BEING PRETTY ISN'T MUCH. I KNOW A LOT OF PRETTY PEOPLE I WOULDN'T TRUST WITH A BUSTED NICKEL-PLATED WATCH. BUT SOME OTHERS, SOMETHIN' COMES OUTTA THE INSIDE OF 'EM AND YOU KNOW YOU CAN TRUST 'EM."

★ ★ ★

—Hondo Lane, *Hondo* (1953)

Good Things Come in Small Packages

Wise men know size isn't always an indicator of quality or value, and it's foolish to dismiss a tool at your disposal simply because it's on the small side—especially when you're at war.

★ ★ ★

I N *THEY WERE EXPENDABLE* (1945), John Wayne plays Lt. "Rusty" Ryan, a member of the U.S. Navy in World War II. Ryan and his commanding officer, Lt. John Brickley (Robert Montgomery), are sent as part of a PT boat unit to defend the Philippines from a Japanese invasion. However, upon their arrival, the local military commanders laugh at their squadron—they don't see how the smaller PT boats can be any use to the operation, and instead relegate their squadron to messenger duty. Ryan and Brickley are frustrated by the circumstances because they know their men and boats can be useful in combat. Eventually the local command acquiesces, and Ryan and Brickley are proven right, as the smaller boats are thoroughly effective at intercepting and sinking the larger Japanese vessels. Though the Japanese eventually overpower them, the film ends with Ryan and Brickley being airlifted out so they can train more men to fight with PT boats.

The moral of the story? You should always consider every tool at your disposal, and you'd be a fool to ignore a helping hand, no matter how small—particularly in a time of need.

John Wayne and Jeffrey Hunter in a scene from *The Searchers* (1956). Director John Ford filmed the movie in Monument Valley.

Sometimes You Need to Use Tough Love

Enacting discipline on those we're closest to in life can be rough. Depending on the severity of the circumstances, one of the consequences we often fear in this situation is the relationship being damaged by lasting resentment. But in many cases, laying down the law is for the greater good.

★ ★ ★

JOHN WAYNE'S Capt. Jim Gordon finds himself in such a position in the 1942 film *Flying Tigers*. Commanding his unit of fighter pilots in China ahead of World War II, Gordon already has the deck stacked against him. To make matters worse, he must contend with the ego of his old friend Woody Jason, a pilot who would rather go into business for

himself to prove a point than work cooperatively within the unit. Beyond being insubordinate, the brash pilot is simply reckless. Recognizing Jason's antics as not just dangerous to himself but also to the Flying Tigers as a whole, Gordon decides to fire Jason.

If Gordon had chosen to give Jason a pass and let his actions slide, there's no telling the harm that could have been done to his unit. It goes to show that no matter the history you may have with someone, no one should be exempt from some necessary tough love.

Most Things Are Black-and-White

> **"THERE'S RIGHT AND THERE'S WRONG.**
> **YOU GOTTA DO ONE OR THE OTHER."**
>
> —COL. DAVY CROCKETT, *THE ALAMO* (1960)

★ ★ ★

N 1960, *The Alamo*, one of the most acclaimed films of Duke's career, was released. As the story goes, Col. Davy Crockett (John Wayne) and Col. Jim Bowie (Richard Widmark) decide to join the fight against the incoming Mexican army. As the enemy is revealed to completely outnumber Crockett and his crew, the options are cut-and-dry. They could retreat, allowing the Mexican army to overtake the Republic of Texas unchallenged. Or they can stand and fight. The choice is clear—and a lasting reminder that in life, you're not likely to find many gray areas between right and wrong.

Pride Can Be Blinding

Being handed a lot of responsibility is challenging, especially when you want to prove yourself as a capable leader. However, there's no shame in listening to advice from those with more experience—in fact, putting your pride before your common sense is a good way to get yourself in a whole lotta trouble.

★ ★ ★

THIS SCENARIO plays out before audiences' eyes in the 1948 film *Fort Apache*, which sees John Wayne's Capt. Kirby York being passed over for a promotion to commander in favor of Henry Fonda's cocksure character Owen Thursday. On one hand, the promotion seems logical due to Thursday's impressive record from the Civil War. What

the new commander lacks, however, is experience dealing with the local Apache tribe—something York has in spades. Ignoring York's warnings, Thursday sends his men into battle with the Apaches, resulting in many deaths—including his own. His overall arrogance and lack of diplomacy eventually cost him his life, while York's is spared due to the longstanding respect he has shown for the Apaches.

Pride can easily be emboldened by a new position of authority, and *Fort Apache* shows just how dangerous that can be. Know when to let go of it.

"THE SUN AND THE MOON CHANGE, BUT THE ARMY KNOWS NO SEASONS."

★ ★ ★

—Capt. Nathan Brittles, *She Wore a Yellow Ribbon* (1949)

Don't Fight the People You Love

**Trying times can bring out an ugly side in anyone.
But when we encounter these types of challenges in life, it's best to
stand beside those closest to us rather than against them.**

★ ★ ★

I N THE 1948 film *Red River*, John Wayne plays Thomas
Dunson, a headstrong cattle rancher who adopts an orphan boy
named Matthew Garth. After starting out with nothing but a
bull and Garth's cow, Dunson eventually manages to assemble a
successful cattle ranch, which requires him to hire more men. But
when financial issues and other hardships arise, Dunson becomes
increasingly tyrannical, causing Garth to reach his breaking point

and rebel with some of the ranch hands. Dunson is enraged and vows to make Garth pay with his life. When the two finally encounter each other, they come to blows until Tess, Garth's love interest, interferes by firing a gun several times and demanding the two come to their senses and stop fighting. The men reconcile, and Dunson later encourages Garth to marry Tess before adding his initial to the ranch's brand as he had promised to do years prior.

When it comes to family, set the fisticuffs aside. Instead, work together to fight the challenges life throws your way (even when those challenges come from the people you love).

Follow Your Heart

★ ★ ★

S HONDO LANE, John Wayne finds himself in an unusual set of circumstances and must pretend to be the husband of homesteader Angie Lowe (Geraldine Page) in order to save his own life. Though she has recently learned her real husband has died, Lowe quickly falls for Hondo, and he for her. Lowe feels guilty for loving another man so soon after becoming a widow, though Hondo assures her that she shouldn't—after all, we can't help how we feel.

With a Little Faith, Anything is Possible

We've all heard confidence is key, a widely applicable maxim that was certainly not lost on John Wayne. Throughout his life and career, the actor's determination and belief in himself led him to overcome the odds and power through to success. The same was true for many of his on-screen characters.

★ ★ ★

S ROBERT HIGHTOWER in the 1948 film *3 Godfathers*, Duke teaches us that truly remarkable feats can be achieved when we keep hope alive. After robbing a bank, Hightower and his fellow outlaws William Kearney (Harry Carey Jr.) and Pedro Roca Fuerte (Pedro Armendáriz) flee into the Arizona desert. Along the way, they encounter a dying woman

in labor and help her deliver the child. The three robbers on the run promise the woman they will ensure the baby boy, named Robert William Pedro after all of them, makes it to safety. The journey becomes extremely perilous and despite losing both Kearney and Fuerte along the way, Hightower continues on. He finally makes it into town with the baby still safe, just as he had promised.

We can't control when the flesh becomes weak. But we are able to keep the spirit willing, and that's what matters most.

You Can Only Rely on Yourself

★ ★ ★

IN *THEY WERE EXPENDABLE*, Duke's character, Lt. "Rusty" Ryan, has a sizable chip on his shoulder, which often results in him butting heads with his superior, Lt. John Brickley. This comes to a head when Brickley refuses to let Ryan help defend against Japanese attacks, believing his unit of PT boats to be unsuitable for combat. Following a surprise attack, however, Brickley's hand is forced, and Ryan proves his worth once and for all. The takeaway from this story? You know what you're capable of, and the only person you can rely on to advocate for you is the man in the mirror.

John Wayne and James Caan on set of *El Dorado* (1967). The film was based on the 1960 novel *The Stars in Their Courses* by Harry Brown.

Judge People for Who They Are

Some say where you've been and what you've done
makes you who you are. While this is true, it doesn't mean
people should be defined by their past.

★ ★ ★

OHN WAYNE'S breakout 1939 film *Stagecoach* features his character, the Ringo Kid, adhering to this notion. While on a stagecoach trip that evolves into the adventure of a lifetime due to the looming threat of Geronimo and his Apaches, the Ringo Kid gets to know the band of strangers he's sharing the ride with. Some of the passengers are flawed in ways more apparent than others, such as Doc Boone (Thomas Mitchell) the heavily intoxicated doctor and the embezzling banker Henry Gatewood (Berton Churchill). One passenger Ringo is quite taken with is Dallas (Claire Trevor), a prostitute who had been ostracized from town. Despite her complicated past, Ringo falls for her quickly. Having escaped jail with plans to kill the man who murdered his father and brother, he recognizes the importance of not judging others.

The passage of time allows for the opportunity to change and grow. The true testament to a person's character is whether they seize that opportunity.

"I DON'T LIKE QUITTERS, ESPECIALLY WHEN THEY'RE NOT GOOD ENOUGH TO FINISH WHAT THEY START."

★ ★ ★

—Thomas Dunson, *Red River* (1948)

Success Requires Hard Work

"NO GREAT TRAIL WAS EVER BUILT
WITHOUT HARDSHIP."

—BRECK COLEMAN, *THE BIG TRAIL* (1930)

★ ★ ★

I N JOHN WAYNE'S first starring role, as Breck Coleman in *The Big Trail*, he explained something simple yet important: Greatness doesn't come from luck, and creating something worthwhile isn't an easy task. In fact, anything worth doing is probably difficult to do. The idea that it takes a lot of grit, determination and effort to make something great isn't a new one, but it is a lesson we can all stand to be reminded of every now and again.

It's Only Failure If You Give Up

We tend to measure success based solely on whether we achieve the goals we set out to conquer. But setbacks are inevitable, and sometimes success is truly measured by how you react to coming up short.

★ ★ ★

 OHN WAYNE'S character Capt. Nathan Brittles in *She Wore a Yellow Ribbon* (1949) is no stranger to setbacks. Between his age beginning to set in and the missions of his troop becoming increasingly difficult, Brittles is eyeing his retirement from the U.S. Cavalry. One of his primary remaining objectives is to avoid escalating a looming American Indian war, which he first attempts to accomplish by trying to personally make peace with Chief Pony-That-Walks. His efforts are unsuccessful, but Brittles is undeterred and steadfast in preventing unnecessary bloodshed. Putting it all on the line, he decides to cause a stampede of the horses at the American Indian camp, which leaves the tribes no choice but to flee to their reservation.

The risk of failure will always be present in life, but it's a risk worth taking. If you quit, you cheat yourself out of the chance to succeed.

And if you stick it out long enough, you just might succeed when it matters most.

A Little Patience Goes a Long Way

"WHERE I COME FROM, WE DON'T SHOOT HORSES WHEN
THEY GET ORNERY; WE TAME 'EM."

—JOHN DRURY, *RIDE HIM, COWBOY* (1932)

★ ★ ★

 N *RIDE HIM, COWBOY*, John Wayne's character John Drury saves a horse on trial for murder by offering to ride him. As it turns out, the horse was framed by the nefarious Henry Sims, known by reputation as the Hawk. When Drury is later tied up by the Hawk and left to die in the desert, the horse comes to his aid—untying the cowboy and saving his life. It goes to show that by practicing patience, we can see things the way they truly are.

Hard Work Prepares You for a Hard Life

There's no way of knowing what kinds of hardships life will throw your way. The only guarantee is that those challenges will come, so it's up to you to build a foundation of grit in order to be prepared.

★ ★ ★

UKE'S SGT. JOHN STRYKER in the 1949 film *Sands of Iwo Jima* is far from beloved among his squad of U.S. Marines. Stryker's training tactics are incredibly intense and unyielding, and his men share a unanimous disdain for him. But once Stryker's squad of Marines step foot on the battlefield in the invasion of Tarawa, they quickly realize the reasoning behind

his tough, no nonsense attitude. The platoon leader is killed immediately while two privates are badly wounded. When the squad eventually enters the Battle of Iwo Jima, more men are lost to the violent chaos, including Stryker himself. With the horrors of war fully revealed, it becomes apparent that Stryker's ruthless approach was his best attempt to prepare the men for what was to come.

The lesson here is that, as grueling as it may be, hard work pays off in many ways. Being unprepared for the unavoidable tough times will only make them worse.

"A MAN OUGHTA DO WHAT HE THINKS IS BEST."

★ ★ ★

— Hondo Lane, *Hondo* (1953)

Cooler Heads Will Always Prevail

When it comes to life or death situations, it's a safe bet that any of John Wayne's on-screen characters would know just what to do in order to get out alive. But for many of us, keeping calm in the event of an emergency is easier said than done.

★ ★ ★

THE 1954 FILM *The High and the Mighty* sees Duke as Dan Roman, the veteran first officer aboard a commercial airliner that develops major mechanical problems on a flight from Honolulu to San Francisco. Despite having previously lost his wife and son in a plane crash—as well as having a permanent limp as a physical reminder of that tragedy—Roman remains calm throughout the potentially deadly flight, doing his

best to ease the fears of the passengers. After it's discovered that the damage to the plane has caused significant fuel loss, Roman's experience tells him they have a better chance at survival if they attempt to make it to land rather than ditching in the ocean. However, the airliner's captain, John Sullivan (Robert Stack), succumbs to panic and attempts to ditch the plane anyway. Roman slaps Sullivan back to his senses, and the pilot is able to keep his cool long enough to take the plane to a safe, albeit miraculous, landing in San Francisco.

Fortunately, most of us aren't likely to find ourselves in such a high-stakes, life-or-death set of circumstances as those seen in *The High and the Mighty*. But the lesson here remains the same: The only chance at making it through a nerve-racking situation is to keep your head clear and stay calm.

John Wayne and Richard Widmark play Davy Crockett and Jim Bowie, respectively, in 1960's *The Alamo*. The film is one of five directed by Duke.

A Man Has to Have a Code

Life is full of forks in the road, and we choose which direction to go based on our own moral compass. Without it, we'd be aimless, prone to heading into dark territory.

★ ★ ★

ESPITE KNOWING for certain there will be professional consequences to suffer, John Wayne's character Capt. Karl Ehrlich in the 1955 film *The Sea Chase* sticks to his moral code. A former career naval officer in Germany, Ehrlich strongly opposes the rise of the Nazi regime. With the outbreak of World War II, Ehrlich's steadfast opposition to his country's Nazi agenda costs him his rank and position. He's then tasked with taking a woman named Elsa Keller (Lana Turner), who may possess valuable war secrets, from Sydney, Australia, back to Germany aboard his ship, the *Ergenstrasse*. When the ship docks at Auckland Island for supplies, Ehrlich's pro-Nazi Chief Officer Kirchner (Lyle Bettger) murders three fishermen. British Commander Jeff Napier (David Farrar) finds the bodies and is convinced his old friend Ehrlich is the culprit; but the anti-Nazi German knows Kirchner is responsible and forces him to sign the ship's log detailing the truth. Eventually, German radio sells out the whereabouts of the *Ergenstrasse* due to Ehrlich's politics, and Napier is able to catch up and sink the ship. After it's too late, *Ergenstrasse* crew members who had already deboarded present the ship's log to Napier, revealing Ehrlich's innocence.

Even when facing intense adversity from his fellow countrymen, Ehrlich never abandons his code. While *The Sea Chase* concludes without revealing whether he survives the sinking of the ship, the film's message is crystal clear: Stand up for what you believe in, no matter the cost.

Take Responsibility

"WELL, THERE ARE SOME THINGS A MAN
JUST CAN'T RUN AWAY FROM."

—THE RINGO KID, *STAGECOACH* (1939)

★ ★ ★

I N HIS BREAKOUT film, *Stagecoach*, John Wayne plays the Ringo Kid, a fugitive looking for vengeance against the man who killed his family. His love interest, Dallas (Claire Trevor), begs him to let it go so they can move on with their lives. But the Ringo Kid knows he'll never rest easy until the score is settled, and explains as much with a line that still resonates. If there's something in your life you know you can't run away from, you're better off facing it head on.

There's Always Another Way

No matter how much you prepare, life will sometimes throw a wrench in your plans. But as long as you have enough grit and determination, you can always pull yourself out of whatever circumstances you find yourself in.

★ ★ ★

N HIS 1957 biographical film *The Wings of Eagles*, John Wayne plays the adventurous Frank "Spig" Wead, a U.S. Navy pilot with an intense passion for bolstering the Navy aviation program. Spig is eventually promoted to fighter squadron commander but before he can step into the new role, he falls down a flight of stairs and becomes paralyzed from the neck down, effectively keeping him from ever flying a plane again. However, Spig realizes there is still a lot left to live for. After months of telling himself, "I'm going to move that toe," he regains movement in his arms and hands, and can even walk with braces and canes. Once his body is able and his spirits are renewed, the Navy asks Spig to write military-related film scripts for Hollywood, a task he excels at. And after the Japanese bomb Pearl Harbor, Spig reenters the service and has the brilliant idea to use "jeep" carriers so downed planes can quickly be replaced.

Though Spig had undoubtedly dreamed of flying those planes himself, he found many other ways to be of service to his country. No matter what your limitations are, there's always a way to achieve your goals—sometimes more than one.

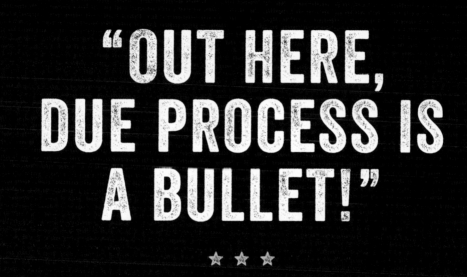

"OUT HERE, DUE PROCESS IS A BULLET!"

★ ★ ★

— Col. Mike Kirby, *The Green Berets* (1968)

Roll with the Punches

You can plan and prep all you want, but life has a funny way of throwing the unexpected our way. And when that happens, the best thing you can do is just accept reality and do your best to deal with the new circumstances.

★ ★ ★

OHN WAYNE'S 1955 film *Blood Alley* features the legend as Capt. Tom Wilder, who finds himself captured and imprisoned after his ship is seized by Chinese Communists. Two years go by before Wilder leaves the confines of the prison, though he exits via unlikely means. The Naval captain is rescued by Chiku Shan villagers, who help him break out of the prison. Wilder soon learns that in exchange for his rescue, the villagers need his help in transporting them to a port in Hong Kong in order to escape Red China. As if the mission isn't already perilous enough, Wilder must make the most of a stolen, dilapidated riverboat and rely on little more than his memory of the coast of China in order to guide everyone to safety. Against all odds, the refugees eventually make it to Hong Kong. It goes to show when things go askew, you still stand a chance to succeed as long as you keep your chin up and carry on.

Never Assume

"NEXT TIME YOU SHOOT SOMEBODY, DON'T GO NEAR
'EM TILL YOU'RE SURE THEY'RE DEAD!"

—COLE THORNTON, *EL DORADO* (1967)

★ ★ ★

N *EL DORADO*, Duke plays Cole Thornton, a rugged gunslinger who heads to the titular town for a job helping rancher Bart Jason wage a ranch war against another family. But once Thornton gets word that his duties might include fighting against his old friend Sheriff J.P. Harrah, he backs out. Months later, after learning Jason has hired a replacement gunman and the sheriff has developed an alcohol problem, Thornton returns to El Dorado. Joined by the wildly inexperienced Mississippi, Thornton has to fend off the enemy while teaching his new sidekick the basics of gunfighting. We soon see Mississippi learn not to assume a bullet equals a fatality, and Jason pay the price for assuming Thornton would let him get away with his nefarious plans. Assuming, as we learn, can be a fatal mistake.

Trust Your Instincts

As legendary as he may be, John Wayne was no psychic. But one thing Duke could do when it came to making tough calls was trust his gut, and many of his characters reveal just how beneficial that practice can be.

★ ★ ★

N HIS 1960 film based on historical events, *The Alamo*, John Wayne plays Col. Davy Crockett, a fearless soldier who joins the fight to prevent Antonio López de Santa Anna and his Mexican army from destroying the new Republic of Texas. From the beginning, the task of stopping the onslaught from the Mexican invaders seems all but insurmountable. Col. William Travis (Laurence Harvey) is assigned by Gen. Sam Houston (Richard Boone) to defend the Alamo in San Antonio while Houston assembles and trains his army. Col. Jim Bowie (Richard Widmark), equipped with a crew of his own, joins Travis and is soon followed by Crockett and his assembly of Tennessean soldiers. The addition of Crockett to the crew quickly proves pivotal— when he senses an imminent attack from Santa Anna and the Mexican army, he sends his youngest defender Smitty (Frankie Avalon) to Houston for reinforcements. In the end, the men defending the Alamo were outnumbered 156 to 7,000. And though the brutal battle was won by the much larger army, Crockett's instincts gave the Texans the best shot they had. When the deck is stacked and you don't have much time to weigh a decision, listen to your instincts.

John Wayne, George Bancroft and Louise Platt in *Stagecoach* (1939). The film was nominated for an Academy Award for Best Picture.

Stubbornness Will Only Get You So Far

When you're leading a team to achieve a goal, it can be tough to avoid a "my way or the highway" mentality. But without being open to the ideas and assistance of others, you're bound to fall short.

★ ★ ★

OHN WAYNE'S Thomas Dunson in the 1948 film *Red River* believes he's clearing a path for his own success, but he's actually creating the roadblocks himself. At first, he has reason to believe he knows best—after starting out with just one bull and one cow, Dunson and his adopted son Matt Garth quickly develop a successful cattle ranch. Dunson eventually hires more ranch hands to relocate and grow the operation, but

the move also sets the stage for trouble. The pigheaded ranch owner becomes impossible to work with as times get tough, lashing out at Garth and the hired hands in both verbally and physically abusive ways. Though Garth tries to reason with him, Dunson is unwilling to hear the concerns of anyone as he only cares about getting his ranch back on track. Finally fed up with the tyranny, Garth and the other ranchers steal the cattle drive right out from under Dunson.

The lesson here? Set stubbornness aside. If you don't work with your team to get ahead, you might be left in the dust.

Apologies Without Actions Are Useless

> ### "'SORRY' DON'T GET IT DONE, DUDE."
> —SHERIFF JOHN T. CHANCE, *RIO BRAVO* (1959)

★ ★ ★

IN *RIO BRAVO*, John Wayne's Sheriff John T. Chance and Dean Martin's Dude get off to a rough start. At the beginning of the film, Chance is disgusted to see Dude in a desperate state of habitual alcohol abuse. Angered and embarrassed, Dude knocks Chance out cold. But after being reminded of Dude's gunslinging skills, Chance deputizes the man under the condition that he stay off the bottle. As Dude struggles to remain sober, he ends up whaling Chance again, for which he quickly says he's sorry. Chance, however, has seen that his "sorry" doesn't mean much. If you want to prove you're truly remorseful, you have to let your actions speak louder than your words.

Do the Right Thing for the Right Reason

It's perfectly healthy to take pride in the good that we've done. Still, it's crucial we don't do those good deeds just for the sake of rewarding our egos.

★ ★ ★

OHN WAYNE as Tom Doniphon and James Stewart as Ransom Stoddard in 1962's *The Man Who Shot Liberty Valance* share the common goal of bringing the outlaw Liberty Valance (Lee Marvin) to justice. Initially, though, they disagree on the means of doing so. Stoddard, an attorney with political aspirations, believes in bringing down Valance via the legal system, while the rugged rancher Doniphon insists the violent wrongdoer can only be stopped by brute force. Realizing he may find himself face-to-face with Valance, Stoddard practices

his marksmanship under Doniphon's tutelage. Stoddard and Valance eventually end up in a standoff, and when the lawyer becomes wounded, he fires a retaliatory shot and Valance falls to the ground, dead. Viewed as a hero by the townspeople, Stoddard is nominated to be a delegate in Washington, D.C., though his belief that he killed a man in a gunfight causes him to reconsider. Doniphon privately reveals to Stoddard that he was actually the one who fired the fatal shot from a nearby alley, assuring Stoddard of his innocence and allowing him to accept the nomination.

Doniphon was never looking for a pat on the back, he simply did what was right by saving Stoddard's life. And by saving his life, Doniphon also saved Stoddard's reputation, as the attorney later had a successful career in government based largely on his accolade of being "the man who shot Liberty Valance." Sometimes, even more good can come from refusing to take credit.

"A MAN'S WORD TO ANYTHING, EVEN HIS OWN DESTRUCTION, IS HIS HONOR."

★ ★ ★

—Col. Kirby Yorke, *Rio Grande* (1950)

Go the Extra Mile for the One You Love

True love doesn't come along all that often and when it does, it's often surrounded by plenty of obstacles. But when you find yourself in a fight for love, you better give it all you've got.

★ ★ ★

JOHN WAYNE'S Air Force Col. Jim Shannon in the 1957 film *Jet Pilot* finds his professional and personal life becoming a tangled web. When Shannon and fellow officer Maj. Rexford (Paul Fix) investigate a Russian jet that has landed in Alaska, they are surprised to see the pilot is a woman named Lt. Anna Marladovna (Janet Leigh) who is seeking refuge.

Shannon is assigned to stick close to Marladovna in the hopes that she'll give up Soviet secrets, but he winds up developing feelings for her. The two spend weeks together, and when Marladovna is about to be deported, Shannon marries her. As it turns out, Marladovna is actually a Soviet spy named Olga Orlief sent to retrieve secrets from unwitting servicemen like Shannon. The controversial newlyweds then travel to Russia, where Shannon will attempt a counter-conspiracy. But Orlief realizes her feelings for Shannon are legitimate, and she no longer wishes to carry out the mission assigned by her homeland. The two flee Soviet Russia in a hijacked jet and make it to the safety of America, where they can begin their new life of freedom together. The story here is centered around a classic lesson in love: It's worth going the extra mile.

John Wayne and Ricky Nelson on set of *Rio Bravo* (1959). The film's sets were built to 7/8 scale, to make the actors seem larger than life.

If You Love Someone, Tell Them

It's no secret that life is short, so we might as well spend the time we're given with the ones we love. But if you suppress your true feelings for someone, you're only wasting precious time that could be lived to the fullest extent.

★ ★ ★

THE 1960 FILM *North to Alaska* features John Wayne as Sam McCord, a man who strikes gold both literally and, as far as his feelings go, figuratively. He travels to Seattle to pick up mining equipment as well as his partner George Pratt's (Stewart Granger) fiancée, Jenny Lamont (Lilyan Chauvin), but discovers that the woman has married another man in Pratt's absence. Concerned for his partner's inevitable heartbreak, McCord decides to bring a hostess named Angel (Capucine) back to meet Pratt. On the boat back to Nome, however, Angel misreads the situation and develops feelings for McCord. The two arrive in Nome and Pratt, unwilling to go along with McCord's idea, schemes to help Angel win McCord's affection. Despite their attempts, McCord doesn't seem to be taking to the woman the way she hopes. But when Angel attempts to board a ship to leave town, McCord insists she stay, declaring, "Because I love you, that's why!" In the end, McCord learns this important lesson in the nick of time: If you bite your tongue for too long, you might miss your chance to tell someone how you really feel.

There's No Time Like Right Now

> **"SLAP SOME BACON ON A BISCUIT AND LET'S GO! WE'RE BURNIN' DAYLIGHT!"**
>
> —WIL ANDERSEN, *THE COWBOYS* (1972)

★ ★ ★

IN *THE COWBOYS,* John Wayne plays Wil Andersen, an aging rancher who has his work cut out for him. After losing his crew to a gold rush, Andersen decides to hire a group of local schoolboys to help him prepare for a major cattle drive. Among many lessons about growing up and taking responsibility is the more pragmatic lesson of productivity. And because he needs to train the boys in short order, Andersen doesn't mince words when imparting the importance of using time wisely to get a job done.

Some Things Need to Be Settled...

There's no way around it—life will do you dirty from time to time. And in certain situations, the only way to right the wrong is to settle the score.

★ ★ ★

OHN WAYNE'S Ringo Kid in the 1939 film *Stagecoach* is out for vengeance, and rightfully so. After breaking out of prison upon learning that his father and brother have been murdered by Luke Plummer (Tom Tyler), the Ringo Kid boards a stagecoach with a group of strangers traveling from Arizona to New Mexico. Along the way, the travelers have

SOME THINGS NEED TO BE SETTLED...

to contend with impending attacks from Geronimo and the Apaches. Additionally, the Ringo Kid's plan for avenging the death of his family is met with serious resistance from Dallas (Claire Trevor), the woman whom he falls for while on the journey. But despite the looming danger posed by the Apaches and the possibility of losing Dallas, he's adamant he will confront Plummer—and when he reaches Arizona, he does just that. Despite being outnumbered by Plummer and his brothers, the Ringo Kid bests the murderer in a gunfight. Closure, in its many forms, is often the only way we can move forward with our lives.

...And Some Things Don't

While there may be plenty of situations where retribution is called for, there are just as many that are best left alone. Sometimes, the best way to settle something is to make peace with it by walking away.

★ ★ ★

THE 1947 FILM *Angel and the Badman* sees John Wayne's Quirt Evans and Gail Russell's Penelope "Penny" Worth in a romance complicated by their different backgrounds. Penny, raised in a nonviolent family, is limitlessly compassionate. For his part, Evans has lived a life of violence and developed a reputation as a shoot-first-ask-questions-later gunman. As their unlikely love develops, Penny often has to halt Evans's reactionary urges to grab his gun and saddle up. But when his rivalry with Laredo (Bruce Cabot) and Hondo (Louis Faust) is reignited, Evans decides he will have to settle things like he always has in order to protect Penny. When he goes to confront his old rivals, however, Penny arrives and convinces him to surrender his gun to her. Laredo and Hondo are then shot by Marshal McClintock before they can do any harm. When Evans's pal Bradley suggests the gunman may need his weapon back, McClintock utters the final line of the film, "Only a man who carries a gun ever needs one." Evans is free to leave his life of violence and conflict behind and pursue a life of peace with Penny, showing us that sometimes, letting go is the best way to move on.

"I KNOW THOSE LAW BOOKS MEAN A LOT TO YOU, BUT NOT OUT HERE. OUT HERE, A MAN SETTLES HIS OWN PROBLEMS."

★ ★ ★

—Tom Doniphon, *The Man Who Shot Liberty Valance* (1962)

Fight for What You Believe In

Strong beliefs require a strong will. There will always be those who don't see eye to eye with you on important matters, and in those situations, you have to be willing to stand up and fight.

★ ★ ★

OHN WAYNE'S Col. Davy Crockett and his assembly of intrepid men in the 1960 film *The Alamo* all share a common belief as well as the willingness to fight for it. Aware of the imminent danger of Antonio López de Santa Anna and his Mexican army overtaking the Republic of Texas, Crockett joins Col. William Travis (Laurence Harvey) in an effort to defend the Alamo in San Antonio at all costs. Awaiting the training and subsequent arrival of a much larger army, the two colonels and their men are vastly outnumbered by the Mexicans. But, because they'd rather die than see the Republic of Texas seized by a foreign tyrant, they're willing to stay and fight until the bitter end. And the end is indeed bitter. But while Crockett and his men are killed in battle, they die without having been defeated mentally. It's a reminder that we must stand by our convictions, even when it means standing up to those who oppose them.

John Wayne and John Agar in *Sands of Iwo Jima* (1949). Duke's fist and footprints outside Grauman's Chinese Theatre contain black sand from Iwo Jima.

In a Crisis, Set Your Differences Aside

Though there may be people in this world who you don't like or trust, wise men will put their differences aside to work together when a bigger threat comes along. Sometimes, doing so will make you realize your original enemies weren't that bad after all.

★ ★ ★

 N 1961's *THE COMANCHEROS*, John Wayne plays the tough, determined Texas Ranger Jake Cutter. Early on in the film, Cutter captures the gambler and outlaw Paul Regret (Stuart Whitman), who is wanted for killing a Louisiana judge's son in a duel. For his part, Regret maintains he shot to injure, not kill, but his dueling partner shifted at the last moment. Regret manages to

escape from Cutter, though he is picked up again after the two happen to walk into the same saloon. However, while Cutter is bringing Regret back to Louisiana to face justice, the pair run into a violent gang known as the Comancheros. Regret seizes the opportunity to jump on a horse, though he quickly returns with more Texas Rangers, effectively saving Cutter. Later, Regret again helps Cutter take down the Comancheros. After having fought together side-by-side, Cutter decides to let Regret go.

While Cutter initially didn't like or trust Regret, he realized he could count on him when their lives were on the line. While you may not find yourself in such a perilous situation, it's still smart to remember that reasonable people will join together when the circumstances call for it.

Do the Right Thing for the Right Reasons

> **"I NEVER SHOT NOBODY I DIDN'T HAVE TO."**
>
> —ROOSTER COGBURN, *TRUE GRIT* (1969)

N *TRUE GRIT*, John Wayne portrays the rough curmudgeon U.S. Marshal Rooster Cogburn. After testifying against an outlaw whom he arrested, a defense attorney tries to make him seem like a loose cannon based on the number of people he has had to kill. But Cogburn holds firm that it's a dangerous job and whenever he shoots to kill, the person deserves it. At the end of the day, Cogburn's just doing what he has to so he can come home safe—and truly, that's the best any of us can do.

Know When to Let Go of the Past

Sometimes people lose in love, and their instinct is to guard their hearts so they can't be hurt again. But as Duke shows us in 1962's Hatari!, this is a mistake—there's a fine line between learning from the past and not being able to move on from it.

S SEAN MERCER, John Wayne is the leader of a group of people who capture wild animals in east Africa. His team needs to be careful to not kill the animals, as they must be sold to zoos at the end of the hunting season. It's not an easy life—catching the creatures is dangerous work, and one of the group's members is seriously wounded by a rhinoceros. Mercer

knows from experience that this job isn't good for his romantic prospects. As the audience eventually discovers, he had been engaged once before, but his fiancée couldn't stand living in those conditions. She left abruptly, and it broke his heart.

Because of his past, Mercer is wary when a photojournalist named Dallas (Elsa Martinelli) joins their group. He seems to be falling for her, and she clearly is attracted to him, but Mercer refuses to admit his feelings for fear of being hurt again. However, when Dallas can no longer stand the frustration and leaves, Mercer finally plucks up his courage. With the help of a few baby elephants, he tracks her down, declares his love and the two marry. It just goes to show that letting go of the past is the only way you can enjoy the present.

"WHEN YOU STOP FIGHTING, THAT'S DEATH."

★ ★ ★

—Breck Coleman, *The Big Trail* (1930)

Know When to Set Emotions Aside

Most of us are fortunate enough to never need to send our friends into battle. But even in less dramatic situations, sometimes you need to put your emotions and relationships aside so the best decisions can be made.

★ ★ ★

EING IN CHARGE of a unit of Marine Corps aviators is never an easy task, and the weight of every decision made is especially heavy during times of war. In 1951's *Flying Leathernecks*, John Wayne plays Maj. Dan Kirby, the uncompromising commander of one such group. His men had been expecting one of their own, Capt. Carl Griffin (Robert Ryan), to assume the position and are disappointed when this didn't turn out to be the case. Griffin is much less strict with the young pilots, including Lt. Blithe, his brother-in-law.

Of course, Kirby isn't being tough because he enjoys it or to make his men miserable—he's doing so because they're at war and they have their orders. He abhors making decisions that send the Marines to their deaths, but there's nothing else to be done about it. Eventually, Griffin realizes this is how he must comport himself as well. He proves this during a battle when he refuses to send support to Blithe—his brother-in-law dies as a result, but Griffin knows he had no other choice. It's a stark reminder that honorable men always choose to do the right thing, no matter how difficult it may prove to be.

Actions Speak Louder Than Words

> **"BIG MOUTH DON'T MAKE A BIG MAN."**
>
> —WIL ANDERSEN, *THE COWBOYS* (1972)

★ ★ ★

HILE CHOOSING the next generation of cowhands in *The Cowboys*, John Wayne's Wil Andersen passes over Cimarron, who is a good rider but has a bad temper and a smart mouth. Andersen refuses to train him until Cimarron later proves his worth by saving one of the boys from drowning. When Cimarron asks for more responsibility, Andersen imparts this sage piece of advice we've all heard a version of before. The boy still had a lot to learn before becoming a man, and tough talk can't make up for that. It's not until the boys avenge Andersen's death that their actions finally measure up to their words.

Duke and Robert Montgomery on set of *They Were Expendable* (1945). Montgomery was an actual PT boat captain in World War II and lent his expertise to the film.

Traditions Build Friendships

Friendship shows itself in many ways—usually involving easy conversation, some cold beers or a shared love of sports and Duke movies. But there's another way to strengthen the bond of camaraderie: a knock-down, drag-out fight.

★ ★ ★

N 1963'S *DONOVAN'S REEF,* John Wayne portrays U.S. Navy veteran Michael "Guns" Donovan, who is friends and former shipmates with Thomas "Boats" Gilhooley (Lee Marvin). The two men share a birthday that they celebrate together each year with a full-on fist fight. Donovan and Gilhooley have fought every year for the past 21 years, and the 22nd turns out to be no different. The two men throw fists and chairs, smash tables and

beer bottles, and effectively trash Donovan's saloon. In fact, it seems the only thing they spare is the good stuff—as Donovan yells at Gilhooley, "Not the brandy, ya dope!" Though neither can remember the event that sparked the annual brawl (it may or may not have had something to do with a dancer named Maybelle), it doesn't matter much since by this point, it's all in good fun.

Though it might not be wise to destroy your place of business in the process, there is something to be said for airing out any light grievances with a scuffle every now and again, or even roughhousing just for the fun of it. As long as there's no real anger behind those punches, that is. And if fighting isn't your thing, find something that is and make an event out of it. Memories, even bitter ones, are what friendships are made of.

"IT ISN'T ALWAYS BEING FAST OR EVEN ACCURATE THAT COUNTS. IT'S BEING WILLING."

★ ★ ★

—J.B. Books, *The Shootist* (1976)

Always Be Prepared

Life's challenges can't always be overcome by sheer strength or grit—you also need to be prepared. thinking about where you want to be and making a plan for getting there is key to coming out on top, no matter the situation.

★ ★ ★

S JACOB McCANDLES, John Wayne plays a gunfighter who has been estranged from his family but returns after his grandson has been kidnapped for ransom in 1971's *Big Jake.* His wife Martha (Maureen O'Hara) has sent for him—she knows getting Little Jake back will be "a harsh and unpleasant kind of business and will require an extremely harsh and unpleasant kind of person to see it through." Along with two

of his sons, Big Jake sets out with the trunk full of ransom money. However, before they can reach the kidnappers, they cross paths with another group intent on stealing their money. In an unpleasant but wise fashion, Big Jake lays a trap for the thieves. They are killed in the fight, though the trunk is also blasted open, revealing only newspaper clippings. As it turns out, Big Jake's strategy was to get his grandson back, and to do it without giving in to the kidnappers' demands—it's a plan he pulls off, too.

Hopefully you never encounter a situation as perilous as the tale of Big and Little Jake, but the lesson can be applied to just about any venture in life. And while it's difficult to foresee every potential outcome coming your way, it's still prudent to get ahead whenever you can. As Duke often showed—whether playing a game of chess or working to save a member of his family—a little planning can go a long way.

Your Word Is Your Bond

**"WORDS ARE WHAT MEN LIVE BY...
WORDS THEY SAY AND MEAN."**

—CAPT. JAKE CUTTER, *THE COMANCHEROS* (1961)

★ ★ ★

I N *THE COMANCHEROS*, after the fugitive Paul Regret saves his life, John Wayne's Capt. Jake Cutter is conflicted. He wants to let the man go so he can avoid the death penalty, but he can't bring himself to do it—after all, he is duty-bound to bring Regret to justice. However, after Regret proves himself by fighting shoulder to shoulder with him for a second time, Cutter decides the best way to honor his word is to let Regret go. After all, it wouldn't serve much justice to send a good man to his death. Similarly, we should all strive to honor our promises in the best ways we can.

Always Look Out for Your Friends

True friends are the ones who are there for you no matter what. That's why, at the end of the day, there are few things as valuable in this world as a friend you can depend on.

★ ★ ★

N 1966'S *EL DORADO*, John Wayne plays gunslinger-for-hire Cole Thornton. Thornton takes a job working for a rancher named Bart Jason (Edward Asner) in the town of El Dorado, but quits as soon as he realizes Jason intends for him to side against Sheriff J.P. Harrah (Robert Mitchum), an old friend of his. Thornton leaves town, but returns a few months later when he hears that Harrah has become a drunk and is about

to run into trouble with a new gunslinger hired by Jason. After getting Harrah to sober up, Thornton helps him defend the town and arrest Jason, though Thornton is later paralyzed and captured by Jason's men. It may seem like Thornton's gotten nothing but trouble for helping his friend, but Harrah agrees to a risky trade—Jason for Thornton—to get the man back. Reunited, Thornton and Harrah are able to dispatch Jason and his men and restore justice to El Dorado.

Both men took big risks to help one another—Thornton returned to a dangerous situation without a second thought and Harrah chanced releasing Jason in order to save Thornton's life. But because they trusted one another, both of these risks paid off. Make friends you know you can rely on no matter what, and that will surely pay off, too.

Everything in Moderation, Including Moderation

"FUNNY THING ABOUT PANCAKES: I LOSE MY APPETITE FOR 'EM AFTER THE FIRST COUPLE O' DOZEN."

—QUIRT EVANS, *ANGEL AND THE BADMAN* (1947)

★ ★ ★

FTER BEING laid up in bed recovering, John Wayne's Quirt Evans has quite an appetite. Six eggs, a pound of sausage and a dozen doughnuts later, he's finally feeling like himself again. Having quite that many is questionable—as his host points out, "What harm can there be in a little doughnut, unless one eats so many of them they explode?" A couple days later, after eating his fill of pancakes, Evans's appetite finally seems to be satisfied, and those big breakfasts have prepared him for a long day's work—something else that can be done in moderation.

John Wayne and Geoffrey Deuel in a scene from *Chisum* (1970). The film is loosely based on events from 1878's Lincoln County War.

Life Won't Always Be Easy

> **"WELL, I GUESS INTO EACH LIFE A LITTLE RAIN MUST FALL."**
>
> —SGT. JOHN STRYKER, *SANDS OF IWO JIMA* (1949)

★ ★ ★

WHILE PREPARING his squad for battle in World War II, John Wayne's Sgt. Stryker fell back on these tried-and-true words. They may have been frustrating for his tired, overworked men to hear, but the truth doesn't care if you're tired: no one promised life would be easy or fair. In fact, sometimes life is decidedly unfair, especially if you're about to invade a Japanese stronghold. In times like these, the only thing you can do is keep going—with luck, the sun will eventually come out.

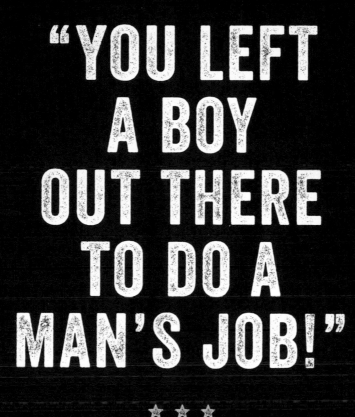

"YOU LEFT A BOY OUT THERE TO DO A MAN'S JOB!"

★ ★ ★

—Cole Thornton, *El Dorado* (1967)

Family Is Everything

As the old saying goes, you can't choose your family.
But you can choose to support them the best way you know how.
Some family members make this more difficult than others,
but when your flesh and blood needs you, you'll know it.

★ ★ ★

 N *BIG JAKE* (1971), John Wayne plays Jacob "Big Jake" McCandles, a skilled gunfighter who has long been estranged from his wife Martha (Maureen O'Hara) and sons Jeff, Michael and James (played by Duke's son, Patrick). His relationship with his sons is strained—Big Jake hasn't seen them since he deserted the family ranch years before. However, when Big Jake receives a letter from Martha asking for his help, he returns home

on the next available train, no questions asked. Upon his return, he learns his son Jeff has been shot and wounded, and that his grandson, Little Jake, has been kidnapped. A lesser man might have left his family again, but Big Jake wastes no time in going after his grandson. He may not have been home for a long while, but he wasn't about to abandon his family when they needed him the most.

Big Jake going to such lengths to save his family went a long way in repairing his bond with both his wife and his sons. You'll likely never need to rescue a family member from a gang of outlaws, but the lesson stands: Family members show up for each other.

Be a Mentor

One of the most valuable things you can give to the next generation is your knowledge. Whether it's your own children or a group of ragtag schoolboys, they'll be better off having learned a little bit of wisdom from you.

★ ★ ★

N 1972'S *THE COWBOYS*, John Wayne plays Wil Andersen, an aging rancher who needs help on his cattle drive after his current ranch hands abandon him to go looking for gold. A local man recommends Andersen train schoolboys for the mission. Andersen considers it, and even goes to the school to meet some of the contenders, but isn't sold on the idea until a bunch of the boys show up for duty at his ranch. It's tough going initially, but ultimately hiring them winds up being the best decision the old rancher could have made. The boys are fast learners (at least, mostly), and by the end of the film, they're fine cowhands and loyal workers. What's more, their teacher has imparted a lot more than the basics of handling cattle—he's taught them how to be men. As Andersen tells them, they've become much more than hired hands and made him proud: "Every man wants his children to be better'n he was. You are."

What's more, mentoring those youngsters didn't just benefit them. It added value to Andersen's life, too. There's nothing quite like knowing the world is a little better because you took the time to pass along the wisdom gained from experience.

"NO MAN IS GONNA MAKE A LIAR OUT OF ME, SIR."

★ ★ ★

—Capt. Kirby Yorke, *Fort Apache* (1948)

Revenge Is Rarely Worth It

It's natural to want justice when we feel we've been wronged, but the circumstances of every wrongdoing are always worth considering. Sometimes the consequences of leaping into action outweigh the satisfaction of exacting payback.

★ ★ ★

N HIS OWN quest for vengeance, John Wayne's Capt. Ralls in the 1948 film *Wake of the Red Witch* eventually pays the price for his clouded judgment. As captain of the *Red Witch*, Ralls is at odds with Mayrant Sidneye (Luther Adler), the owner of the vessel's shipping company. The rivalry revolves around a woman, Angelique (Gail Russell), whom Ralls feels was stolen away from him by Sidneye. In a reckless

act of revenge, Ralls intentionally sinks the *Red Witch*—
allowing the millions of dollars worth of gold onboard to
plummet into the sea with it. The two men later agree on a
deal to share the gold in exchange for Ralls's cooperation in
recovering it, but the mission is revealed to be more perilous
than previously believed. Ralls ends up being the only one
willing to dive into the wreckage, and he is trapped by debris
and killed in the process.

By going to such great lengths to seek revenge, Ralls
creates even bigger problems in his life before losing it
altogether. The lesson is simple: Revenge is a thirst better
left unquenched.

It's OK to Be Afraid

> **"ALL BATTLES ARE FOUGHT BY SCARED MEN WHO'D RATHER BE SOMEPLACE ELSE."**
>
> —CAPT. ROCKWELL TORREY, *IN HARM'S WAY* (1965)

★ ★ ★

S NAVAL CAPT. Rockwell "Rock" Torrey in the film *In Harm's Way*, John Wayne portrays a man who is more than willing to take a few risks to defend his country. After the Japanese attack Pearl Harbor, Torrey's gutsy response initially gets him removed from his commanding post. But when the Navy needs someone to lead a dangerous mission, they turn to Torrey for the job. He's a courageous leader, but he'd correct you if you called him fearless. As he knows, there's nothing wrong with being afraid. You just can't let that be an excuse for avoiding what needs to be done.

Never Underestimate Anyone

"Never judge a book by its cover" is a cliché, and for good reason—a lot of the time, looks don't mean anything. And you're especially foolish if you think someone's not up to the task based solely on their age or appearance.

★ ★ ★

N 1969'S *TRUE GRIT*, a film that really drives this point home, John Wayne plays the iconic Rooster Cogburn, a U.S. marshal said to have, well, "true grit." Early in the film, Cogburn is hired by a young girl named Mattie Ross (Kim Darby) to track down her father's killer. Carrying out this mission leads him to cross paths with the outlaw "Lucky Ned" Pepper (Robert Duvall), a man who makes the fatal mistake of underestimating Cogburn. When

Cogburn asks Lucky Ned if he'd rather be killed right there or surrender peacefully, the outlaw says that's "bold talk for a one-eyed fat man." As it turns out, the words weren't all that bold—the skirmish ends with Cogburn having mortally wounded Lucky Ned and killing two of his men where they stood, not to mention killing the man who killed Mattie's father and saving her from a pit full of rattlesnakes. Of course, he had a little help, but he also had a whole lot of grit.

If that weren't enough, the final scene of the film shows Cogburn jumping a four-rail fence on his horse after Mattie teases him for being too old and fat to pull it off. It just goes to show that you never really know what people are capable of until they show you.

When You Can, Relax

★ ★ ★

S TOM DONIPHON in *The Man Who Shot Liberty Valence*, John Wayne comes upon Ranse Stoddard (James Stewart) in desperate need of help; he's been robbed, whipped and left for dead by the town scourge, Liberty Valance. Doniphon acts quickly and brings Stoddard into town, where he can be treated for his injuries. When Stoddard tries to sit up, Doniphon cautions him to take it easy. In general, a wise man saves his strength for when he really needs it—and definitely takes a moment to recuperate after getting the tar beaten out of him.

"DON'T SAY IT'S A FINE MORNING OR I'LL SHOOT YA."

★ ★ ★

—G.W. McLintock, *McLintock!* (1963)

John Wayne helps Victor McLaglen on set of *The Quiet Man* (1952). Hollywood producers first thought the movie was a "silly Irish story that won't make a penny."

Media Lab Books
For inquiries, call 646-838-6637

Copyright 2019 Topix Media Lab

Published by Topix Media Lab
14 Wall Street, Suite 4B
New York, NY 10005

Printed in China

ISBN 10: 1-948174-09-X
ISBN 13: 978-1-948174-09-1

Cover: ScreenProd/Photononstop/Alamy; 2 Silver Screen Collection/Getty Images; 4 Camerique/Getty Images; 7 Pictorial Press Ltd/Alamy; 9 Album/Alamy; 15 Everett Collection; 21 Album/Alamy; 22 Michael Ochs Archive/Getty Images; 24 Pictorial Press Ltd/Alamy; 27 Everett Collection; 35 Collection Christophel/Alamy; 36 John Springer Collection/Corbis/Getty Images; 43 Everett Collection; 50 Everett Collection; 53 AF Archive/Alamy; 54 Everett Collection; 60 AF Archive/Alamy; 62 Sunset Boulevard/Corbis/Getty Images; 64 Photo 12/Alamy; 67 Collection Christophel/Alamy; 68 TCD/Prod.DB/Alamy; 72 Sunset Boulevard/Corbis/Getty Images; 75 Argosy Pictures Corporation/Ronald Grant Archive/Alamy; 76 Photo 12/Alamy; 81 Everett Collection; 82 Everett Collection; 85 Warner Bros/Photofest; 87 Warner Bros/Photofest; 88 Silver Screen Collection/Getty Images; 90 Everett Collection; 93 Everett Collection; 95 Everett Collection; 99 Collection Christophel/Alamy; 100 Warner Brothers/Getty Images; 102 Everett Collection; 105 Collection Christophel/Alamy; 108 ScreenProd/Photononstop/Alamy; 111 Everett Collection; 117 TCD/Prod.DB/Alamy; 118 AF Archive/Alamy; 121 AF Archive/Alamy; 123 Ronald Grant Archive/Alamy; 126 Entertainment Pictures/Alamy; 129 R.K.O. Radio Pictures/Sunset Boulevard/Corbis/Getty Images; 130 Warner Bros. Pictures/Sunset Boulevard/Corbis/Getty Images; 132 © 20th Century Fox/Everett Collection; 135 © 20th Century Fox/Everett Collection; 137 AF Archive/Alamy; 145 Collection Christophel/Alamy; 146 Sunset Boulevard/Corbis/Getty Images; 148 ScreenProd/Photononstop/Alamy; 151 PictureLux/The Hollywood Archive/Alamy; 155 Album/Alamy; 161 Everett Collection; 163 Paramount Pictures/Sunset Boulevard/Corbis/Getty Images; 164 ©20th Century Fox/Everett Collection; 166 Photo 12/Alamy; 169 Collection Christophel/Alamy; 170 Stanley Bielecki Movie Collection/Getty Images; 176 Everett Collection; 183 Keystone Pictures USA/Alamy; 184 PictureLux/The Hollywood Archive/Alamy; 187 Everett Collection; 190 Everett Collection; 192 Michael Ochs Archives/Getty Images; 196 Photo 12/Alamy; 201 TCD/Prod.DB/Alamy; 202 Stanley Bielecki Movie Collection/Getty Images; 205 Photo 12/Alamy; 206 Collection Christophel/Alamy; 209 Everett Collection; 215 PictureLux / The Hollywood Archive / Alamy; 218 AF Archive/Alamy; 220 Everett Collection; 222 Silver Screen Collection/Getty Images; Back Cover: Ronald Grant Archive/Alamy

JOHN WAYNE
ENTERPRISES